650 | The Kids are Alright

Edited by Edward McCann

650 | WHERE WRITERS READ

Founder / Editor • Edward McCann
Executive Producer • Richard Kollath
Literary Ombudsman • Steven Lewis
Chief of Operations • Jane Kaupp
Technical Advisor • Conrad Trautmann
Technical Advisor • Stephen Kaupp
Director of Communications • Gretchen Reed
Director of Photography • Kevin O'Connor
Videography/Photography • Adley Atia
Chief Audio Engineer • Jesse Chason
Copy Editor • Kathleen Stanley
Graphic Designer • Diane Fokas
Production Director Emeritus • Gregory Bray

Production Assistants
Christopher Dennison, Diane Fokas, Mackenzie Meeks,
Jackie Mercurio, and Brian Reagher

Editorial Committee
Rachel Aydt, Laura Shaine Cunningham, Angela Davis-Gardner,
Joseph Goodrich, Steven Lewis, David Masello, and Honor Molloy

For all the kids, and anyone who ever was one.

ABOUT 650

Raising a child is hard, but so is being a kid, and the road for both parents and children alike is lined with countless rites of passage: First tooth. First day of pre-school. Last diaper change. First lost tooth. Later, there are PTA meetings and ER visits, sibling rivalries and braces, bullies, the birds and bees, puppy love, tough love, driving tests, SAT exams, and—if all goes well—an empty nest. These stories presented in these pages are woven through with an underlying thread of hope that, no matter what challenges they encounter, the kids will be alright.

650 is a celebration of writing and the spoken word—a literary forum featuring two-page, 650-word personal stories that can be performed in five minutes. Our events at theaters, colleges, and libraries in and around New York City are organized around single, broad topics that invite a range of expression, and recorded performances are added to a digital archive of writers reading their work aloud. The writers and their work receive additional exposure through podcasts, broadcasts, our YouTube channel, and in these printed volumes. The volume you hold in your hands is a curated collection from a select group of writers featured at a live reading at the New Rochelle Library in New York's Westchester County.

650 features graduate students and grandmothers, first-timers and bestsellers. It's all about the writing, with an emphasis on craft. It's about the choice of one word over another, about the shape of sentences and paragraphs, the arc of a narrative, the poetry of a unique literary voice. If you love language and enjoy a good story, you've come to the right place. To submit your work or attend our shows, visit our website or Facebook page, and join our mailing list. Please tell your friends about us, and spread the word about the spoken word.

Please tell your friends about us, and **spread the word about the spoken word.**

Ed McCann

Edward McCann, Founder / Editor

READ650.COM
FACEBOOK.COM/READ650

CONTENTS

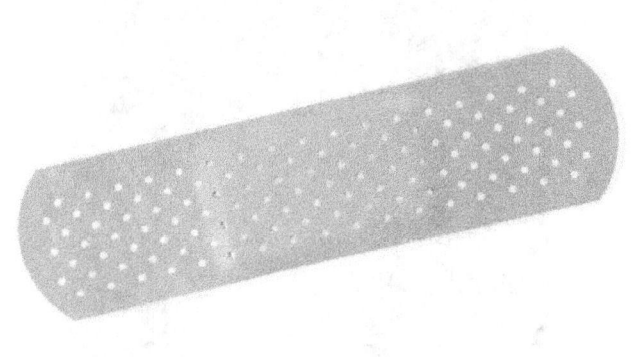

650 | The Kids are Alright

Edited by Edward McCann

PAULA FUNG

Paula Fung lives in a charming neighborhood just north of New York City, with her husband, three daughters, and their dog Boomer. She produces a show on public access television, *Rye Views*, and writes personal essays on the things she knows, which are, in no particular order, cooking, sailing, and family life. Her work has been published on the blog *Sailing Anarchy*.

NAVIGATING

Paula Fung

My sixteen-year old daughter was learning to drive and, to my surprise, I was truly enjoying the process. I was not afraid for our safety, which is unusual, because I avoid adventures of all types. My idea of a thrill is swiping the little pillows off the first class airline seats on my way to coach.

In our encapsulated Subaru-blue world, Emily was especially well behaved. She was very cautious, her eyes didn't leave the road, and she did not even ask to turn on the radio. Our cell phones were turned off and stowed in the glove compartment. As a show of confidence, I crossed my leg and commented on the passing scenery, hoping to telegraph just how relaxed I felt.

Emily asked, "Why do I need the turn signal when I'm already in a turning-only lane?" I told her it's good citizenship to make your intentions known. I told her lack of clarity might be construed as a hidden agenda. I told her this could cause confusion and sometimes even grief.

Privately, I recalled the middle school "cheating incident."

When she was in seventh grade, I received a tearful phone call from Emily saying her science teacher had accused her of cheating on an exam. The call-waiting signaled, and on the other line the teacher herself informed me I needed to meet her at the guidance office. I sped across town and entered the school where some of Emily's friends passed me in the hall, giving me the big eyes.

In the office of her guidance counselor, my strong and stoic child was nearly incoherent. Scientific formulas were inked in bold black Sharpie on both hands and up the inside of her left arm. Her explanation was that she did it to "study."

I often did the exact same thing for the subjects that gave me the most trouble, those that called for rote memorization rather than understanding content. Written on my skin, the incomprehensible became part of me for a day or two, and would adhere just long enough to get through the test. I never suggested that Emily do this, but her instinct to do so was completely familiar to me.

On the day of the cheating incident, Emily had worn a short-sleeved shirt; she did not try to hide the marks or wash them off at the lab sinks in the classroom. I told the teacher that I didn't believe she intended to cheat; she was just very careless in not washing off the ink. However, I agreed that my daughter was clearly guilty of the appearance of impropriety. Her carelessness alone warranted the test grade of zero, the punishment the teacher planned. My response did not satisfy the teacher. She really wanted me to admit that my daughter was cheating and seemed to want to punish me as well as Emily.

She suggested that Emily was trying to meet the "too high" expectations of her "overly invested" parents. I didn't buy it. Although she was only thirteen years old, we had not yet seen any sign of her doing anything solely to please her parents, her teachers, or her peers. And so Emily received the zero and spent the rest of the marking period trying to make up for it on the remaining labs, quizzes, and tests.

And three years later, from the passenger seat of the Subaru, I wished I could warn her of the roadblocks ahead, of the jug handles, the confusing twists and turns she will likely encounter on the road ahead. But recognizing her growing confidence, I remained quiet, watched her adjust the seat and mirrors to her own fit, and drive us home.

JOSEPH BURGO

Joseph Burgo is a clinical psychologist in private practice and the author of both self-help books and novels. His essays have appeared in the *New York Times*, *The Atlantic*, and other major publications; a recognized expert on narcissism, he is frequently quoted in *USA TODAY*, *Glamour*, the *Huffington Post*, and other major news outlets. He writes a blog on the topic of shame and discusses personality development issues on his website *After Psychotherapy*.

FORETELLING YOUR CHILD'S FUTURE

Joseph Burgo

By the time my oldest son William turned seven, he'd accumulated several hundred dollars in a bank account—cash gifts from relatives at Christmas or on his birthday. Each year after depositing those funds, we'd ask him whether there was anything he'd like to buy. At age seven, he answered the way he always did. "No, there's nothing I want."

"It's your money to do with as you like," I urged him. "Isn't there some toy you want to buy with that money Grandpa sent?" He shook his head. "You're sure?"

We were sitting on the gray leather sofa in our den, Will in his flannel PJs and me in my robe. Looking quite serious, he finally explained: "I'm saving up to buy my children food and clothing."

I've told this story many times over the years, in part because it's funny but also because it seemed to capture something essential about Will—the serious, hyper-responsible child who even at age seven had his eye on the future. Most parents have these stories they like to tell about their kids, part of family lore trotted out at holiday dinners. For many years, that story about Will seemed prescient.

During my own childhood, I often heard my mother tell one particular story about me. According to Mom, my first spoken words came late; when I finally did begin to speak, it was in complete sentences rather than baby talk. Years later, my analyst had a field day with that story, making interpretations about my precocity, my pseudo-maturity, my hatred of being small and inexperienced.

I think that story also says something about my love of language. I wrote a three-chapter "novel" when I was in fourth grade, all about my teacher's pet dragon Herman, and I've been writing ever since. Here I am at age 62, many books and novels later, reading you words that mean so much to me — their music, the quality of the thought behind them.

I also have a favorite story about my second son Paul, who was 10 at the time. We were all in a swimming pool and Will was ridiculing Paul for his latest obsession, some popular new device or trendy article of clothing he wanted us to buy him.

"Why do you always have to have the latest thing?" Will asked.

Paul replied, without a hint of irony, "You have to understand that I am all about trademarks and appearances."

We've teased Paul mercilessly over the years about that remark — unfairly, as if his preoccupation with appearances is merely superficial. With an artist's eye for beauty, he began sculpting the female body at age 12. He later developed an interest in fashion, then independently applied for and won a scholarship to an arts high school in California. Last year, he graduated from Central St. Martin's in London and now works as an assistant designer at Oscar de la Renta.

As Will moved into his late teens and early twenties, he continued to focus on accumulating wealth but seemed less concerned about those hypothetical children. At the University of Chicago, he developed Libertarian views and a Darwinian take on the world. Dog eat dog, the poor and disadvantaged as losers in an evolutionary struggle to survive. When he graduated and began to earn money, he still disliked spending it and saved $40,000 during his first year at Google.

I recently asked him what he intended to do with all his wealth.

He thought about it for a moment. "I'd like to have a lake house one day," he said.

My partner and I have a house not far from several lakes in Colorado and Will shows little interest in visiting us there. "Really?" I asked in surprise.

"There needs to be a place where the whole family can get together," he explained. "If I don't have that after you're gone, who will?"

KAREN DUKESS

Karen Dukess has been a tour guide in the former Soviet Union, a newspaper reporter at the *St. Petersburg Times* in Florida, and the founding features editor of *The Moscow Times* in Russia. She has written book reviews for *USA Today* and blogged about raising teenage boys at *theblunderyears.com* and the *Huffington Post*. Her narrative non-fiction has appeared in *Intima* (Columbia University) and her short story, *Fancy Hat*, appeared in the 2017 issue of the *Westchester Review*. She is a speechwriter at the UN Development Programme and is a member of the Terzo Piano writer's group. She lives in Pelham, New York.

MAMA BEAR

Karen Dukess

While planning our family horseback, fly-fishing pack trip along the Soda Fork River in Wyoming, a friend who stalks elk with a bow and arrow there reacted to the news of my adventure with two words: bear spray. I bought four canisters.

Reading the instructional pamphlet, I learned that when a bear charges, you must 1) grab the bear spray that you keep at the ready in a holster on your belt 2) flip the orange tab at the top and 3) pointing slightly downward because grizzlies lower their heads when they attack, wait until the bear is 15 to 20 feet from pulverizing you to push the button and diffuse a cloud of intense pepper spray in its face.

The pamphlet also informed me that the worst kind of grizzly to encounter is a Mama Bear with cubs; her instinct to protect her young is immediate and ferocious.

I was too afraid to practice using the spray the recommended seven times, or even once, so I held onto a glimmer of faith that if I came face to face with a grizzly, my maternal instinct would kick in and enable me to fire the bear spray effectively enough to save me and my sons.

One evening just before dusk, I was walking through the scratchy, waist-high bushes between the bends of the Soda Fork with my 16-year-old son, Johnny. He had a fly rod in his hand and a canister of bear spray hooked to his quick-dry pants. Watching his long strides through the bushes, I realized our best chance of surviving no longer relied on me. I still had the maternal desire to protect him, but only Johnny had the confidence and quick reactions to save us.

We had apparently reached a mother-son crossroads—he on the way up, me on the way down—that made child's play of events I had taken for milestones: his starting to shave, his learner's permit, his first girlfriend. I had no doubt that if we were under attack, Johnny wouldn't turn to me for protection, but would come to my aid.

This shift made me feel safe, and a little sad. It was a natural progression, following years of rejoicing in my sons' physical growth, of charting their height in pencil on the basement door and sharing their pride when the notches climbed higher and higher, of smiling to myself when I had to ask one of them to reach a platter on a top shelf. It was also a reminder that as my boys got older, so would I.

Standing up to my ankles in the cool, clear waters of the Soda Fork, I watched Johnny cast his fishing line in wide loops and then drop his fly like a gentle raindrop on a dark riffle at the river's edge. He let it drift and then pulled the line up and cast again. The fly floated down river without a nibble. Johnny reeled it in and walked a few steps further upstream, where he cast his line toward a log partly submerged in the water. Dwarfed by the thousands of fir trees and pine trees across the river, and the vast, craggy mountains above, Johnny was focused and silent. He cast, and drifted, and reeled and cast again. He seemed unaware of my presence.

I glanced back toward our campsite, thinking we should head back before it started to get dark. As I was checking to make sure my bear spray was secure in my pocket, Johnny shouted, "Got one!" I turned and saw his rod bend into a u-shape as he pulled it back and started to reel in. The fish splashed and Johnny grabbed the line to pull from the water a fat brown trout. Johnny turned toward me, like a compass swinging north, with a huge boyish smile. It was a good catch.

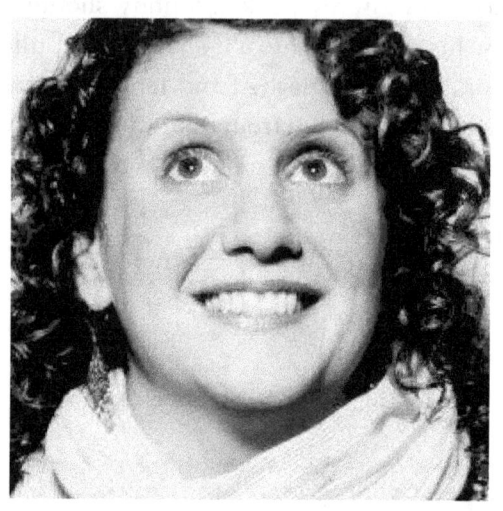

HONOR FINNEGAN

Honor Finnegan has been singing and performing since she was a child. She was in the first national tour of *Annie*, she performed at the Improv Olympic, Chicago's premiere venue for improvisational comedy, and she's won accolades for singing and for folk music songwriting. On May 29th, 2016, Honor had a near-death experience when she was swept away in her car during a flash flood in Texas while at the Kerrville Folk Festival. Weeks later, she wrote and performed a story about that experience at *The Moth* and has been writing more stories ever since.

MR. CLEAN

Honor Finnegan

I'm a cultural Catholic. That's all the shame, and none of the fun.

When I was seven years old, and attending weekly Sunday mass, to which we were always late, my mother said, "You can go up now." That was it. My first communion. No white dress. No celebration. No visit to the forbidden, fascinating confessional.

I loved church because it embodied two of my great loves: God, and the theatre. The mass was pure drama. Cool costumes, great stories, ritual steeped in meaning, incense, singing, and don't forget the Catholic line dance; sit, stand, kneel, and a sit stand, kneel, all together now.

Of course we shouldn't have too much fun. Christ had died for our sins. Let us never forget.

In 1991, I moved to Ireland to find an Irish husband, and married an Englishman. Life is full of the unexpected.

After a 38-hour labor, I became mother to one baby boy. Chubby, sturdy, and bigger than my 5'1" frame should have carried, he looked like Mr. Clean.

He was the apple of my eye. I wanted to celebrate.

Perhaps a baptism was in order. When in Ireland ...

My husband, the atheist, wasn't having it. I understood his reservations. I wasn't a practicing Catholic. I didn't believe in original sin. I knew the church was full of corruption and wrongdoing, but it felt like this major event should be ritualized, recognized in some official way.

I didn't have the strength to organize a hippie alternative, and frankly, I didn't want one. I wanted the real deal.

My husband won. He didn't get the heartfelt part of religion. I couldn't make him understand. I let it go.

Before my son could even walk, he was always on the go. "Ha," he'd say crawling on his hands and knees, meaning, "hat," meaning, "I want to go out. Get me my hat."

So, when he started walking it was our duty to make a way for him to get his exercise.

When it was raining in Galway, which was about 90 percent of the time, the options were limited. There were two indoor the shopping centers, dozens of pubs, and a couple of churches.

On one such rainy day, I took his toddling self over to Our Lady Assumed Into the Heavens Cathedral not far from our house on Nun's Island. It was the big church in Galway, and it was a decent place to let a kid walk about. There was a pretty large car park surrounding it, and you could still be around other people without the smoke of the pub or the bustle of a shopping center. All in all, a pretty chill hang.

After we wandered inside a bit, and lit the obligatory candle or two, we headed back out the entrance. My son ran ahead of me, as toddlers are want to do, and before I knew he was tearing down the wheelchair ramp in his soft, little footies. I was too far away to catch him, and I watched, as he headed to the bottom of the ramp with a bright smile on his face, and a car headed straight for him.

14

I was frozen.

He stopped at the bottom, swayed on his baby legs, then turned around, and smiled back up at me. The car passed, and turned out of the parking lot, onto the main road. I don't think the driver ever saw him.

It all happened so fast. He was inches away. It would have been fatal, I'm sure.

Jesus.

My heart.

My Mr. Clean baptized.

In the name of the Father, and of the Son, and of the Holy Spirit.

Jesus.

MARILYN OGUS KATZ

Marilyn Ogus Katz taught in an educational opportunity program at Purchase College, State University of New York, and then served for many years as dean of studies at Sarah Lawrence College. She left academia to write, primarily fiction, and what had for Marilyn always been an exciting illicit activity became a committed relationship with all of its joys and frustrations. She completed a novel, *The Old City*, about a family of Latvian Jews caught between Hitler and Stalin in 1940 and 1941, and a collection of linked short stories, *A Few Small Stones*, about coming of age in an extended immigrant family in New York City during the 1940s. Her agent has submitted both the novel and short story collection to publishers. Her essays on Wordsworth, the teaching of writing, issues in higher education, and the concerns of older women have appeared in journals and anthologies.

MY DAUGHTER'S HAIR

Marilyn Ogus Katz

My daughter asks me to cut her hair. She spreads towels on her bathroom floor, drapes one over her shoulders and places a chair opposite the mirror. She was always a neat and careful child, but now she's forty-eight and wants a haircut because she has begun chemotherapy. I suggest we wait. She still looks like herself. I think we should hold on as long as we can.

"I'm already seeing hair on my pillow every morning. I don't want to have to deal with hanks of it," she says, her tone even, matter-of-fact.

Her hair began going gray a few years ago and she dyes it brown. When she was an infant, it was dark blond, except for a single pale yellow strand at her tiny neck. As a young mother, I curled that strand around my forefinger again and again, astonished that anything of mine could feel so fine and look so fair.

Over the years, Emily and I fought about her hair. It was one of our issues. I wanted her to keep it long, softer, and more feminine, but she's a rider, skier, and runner, and prefers it close to her head. At sixteen she allowed her hair to grow below her shoulders. It looked lovely. She scheduled a trim. We were meeting for lunch, but as I was about to leave for the restaurant, the phone rang.

"Mom, I wanted to warn you so you don't get upset when you see me. I'm sick and tired of taking care of my hair. I had it cut very short and I think it looks great."

"It's *your* hair, Emily. Do whatever you want with it."
I hung up, called my best friend and ranted for several minutes about what a terrible thing Emily had done. What was wrong with her? Didn't she want to look pretty?

"Marilyn," my friend said. "You sound crazy. You talk as though Emily permanently disfigured herself."

Today I will try for what we used to call a pixie cut, layered and close to the head, the very cut I always hated. I lift one section at a time like the professionals do and snip off an inch. Soon I have exposed Emily's small, flat ears.

"You have such nice ears," I say because there's so much else I can't say.

Clumps float down to the towels. I suffer the loss of each one. When Emily's hair grows back many months from now, it will never again look like the hair of a healthy middle-aged woman. And she always looked younger. In a photo snapped only two years ago, surrounded by her college students in Beginning Latin, it's hard to tell who is the teacher. That same summer she was diagnosed with a rare cancer: sub-dermal t-cell lymphoma. Despite bi-weekly infusions she integrated into her teaching schedule, the disease progressed. Angry red lumps appeared on her slender arms and legs and she began running a fever. She needed aggressive chemotherapy and was forced to take a leave of absence.

I hover over my daughter and catch our heads reflected side by side in the bathroom mirror. My own mop, now salt and pepper, is still thick enough to get compliments. I admit to being vain about it, but suddenly having this much hair at my age seems almost obscene.

"So what do you think?" I ask, careful to place the scissors back in its proper drawer.

"You're a great hairdresser, Mom," Emily exclaims, turning her head, a perfect sphere. "I'm recommending you to all my friends." Competent and brisk, she whips the towel from her shoulders, gathers the others and shakes them into a garbage bag.

I study the wisps framing her delicate face.

"After this is all over," she announces. "I'm keeping my hair short."

JOHN GREDLER

John Gredler poet and memoirist, has been writing prodigiously in notebooks and journals for most of his adult life. He honed his craft at the Writing Institute at Sarah Lawrence College, Bella Villa Writers, 125, and the Terzo Piano Workshops. Published in *Fictionique, Narratively, Dan's Papers, Westchester Review,* and *Talking Writing,* John's essay, "Glistening Scar," won top prize in the Talking Writing Nature Writing contest, and he was awarded the 2014 Gurfein Fellowship from the Writing Institute at Sarah Lawrence College. John lives and writes in Tuckahoe, New York.

QUANTICO

John Gredler

We'd never been on a long trip anywhere so when we took the train to Grand Central and walked over to the Port Authority I was excited. Going through the Lincoln Tunnel on the bus scared me though, all I could think of was all that water on top of us. On the Turnpike the thump thump of the bus tires on the pavement put me into a deep sleep, my face against the window. When I woke I didn't know where I was, my cheek stuck to the glass with my drool.

It was a month after dad ran off with Mrs. White. Mom said we were going to visit the Vaughts in Quantico, Virginia, for a few days. Mr. Vaught was a Major in the Marines, he had just shipped out to Vietnam. Irene was Mom's best friend.

When got off the bus in Washington Mom hired a taxi to take us around. First to the Lincoln and Jefferson Memorials. From there we went to the Capitol and then to the Tomb of the Unknown Soldier and to President Kennedy's grave. I wondered how the flame could stay lit like that even if it rained. Mom knelt right down on the stone and cried.

By the time we got to the Iwo Jima Memorial we were all pretty tired. The four of us kids posed for a picture, none smiling. Mom's heel broke and she skinned her shin on the high curb of at the base of the monument. She cursed and then she was crying again. We stood around her watching blood ooze from her shin.

In Quantico the Vaughts were living in a little house on the Marine Base. It wasn't what I thought it would be. No soldiers with guns or tanks. Just lots of these little houses that all looked the same. There were no trees and hardly any grass.

Behind the house a ways was the Potomac River. The four of us walked down to the water with Kevin and Mike Vaught. The river was brown and the bank was flat dried mud that seemed to go on and on. I went off with Kevin to collect bottles. We lined them up on a top of a rusty old refrigerator, throwing rocks until we broke them all.

The others kept walking along the river. They found an unopened quart can of Hawaiian Punch and thinking it a great treasure carried it all the way back to the house to show our moms. Mrs. Vaught threw it in the garbage.

The next day Mom and Irene were huddled over their cups of tea in the kitchen, blue smoke from their Salems filling the room. After we had our bowls of cereal they told us to go outside. Down the street there was a small playground with a set of swings and a crooked slide. My sister Jeanne got on the one good swing and wouldn't get off. We all yelled at her to let us have a turn. She just kept swinging, not looking at anyone, ignoring us. Finally she jumped off and I got on. She ran into the house and came back out with Mom.

—Let your sister have a turn.

—She was just on it for like an hour.

—Let her have a turn now.

—But she just got off.

Mom grabbed the chain jerking the swing to a stop.

—Go in the house now.

I ran into the bedroom and climbed onto the top bunk, I lay there pounding the wall. I hate you I hate you I hate you I said over and over. My mother came in.

—So, you hate me?

—I hate her, I said.

We both knew I was lying.

Turning to face the wall again I started crying. I couldn't stop. I buried my face in the blankets, my shoulders shaking. When I turned around again Mom was gone.

STEVEN LEWIS

Steven Lewis, Literary Ombudsman for 650, is a columnist at Talking Writing, and a member of the Sarah Lawrence College Writing Institute faculty. A longtime freelancer, his work has been published in *The New York Times, The Washington Post, Christian Science Monitor, the Los Angeles Times, Ploughshares, Spirituality & Health* and others. His novels include Take This and Loving Violet, both from Codhill Press, and Finishing Line Press published Steve's poetry chapbook, *If I Die Before You Wake.* His backlist includes *Zen and the Art of Fatherhood, The ABCs of Real Family Values, The Complete Guide for the Anxious Groom,* and *Fear and Loathing of Boca Raton* (a Hippie's Guide to the New Sixties). He divides his time between his writing space in New Paltz, New York, and Hatteras Island, North Carolina.

ELEVEN WHISKEY SOURS

Steven Lewis

Five of us, home on our first Christmas break from college, tumble down the steep steps at the Village Vanguard like we're the cherries in the whiskey sour of life.

Moments later, the small round table right in front of the stage is crowded with mixed drinks: rum and cokes, 7 and 7s, whiskey sours.

After a second round of drinks, Mose Allison steps up on the stage, places his fingers on the ivories, softly croons "Your mind is on vacation and your mouth is workin' overtime."

And so it goes with the third round of drinks, the mouths of some middle-aged squares at the next table begin workin' overtime. Loudly. Ray swings around and shushes them. They sneer like he's some kind of punk kid and go on talking. Two songs later, growling like someone's father, Michael tells them to shut the hell up. They don't. By the fifth round, Elaine hisses at them.

The sixth, seventh, and eighth rounds appear … and disappear.

As you might guess, given my slightly elevated blood alcohol content at the time, I am guessing that Jane is eleven whiskey sours in when she leans her head on my shoulder, turns her cheek onto my chest and I feel a warm wetness from nipples to crotch—a pool of partially digested maraschino cherries and orange slices in my lap.

That is not all: Michael sees Jane, gags, stands up and barfs on the table.

That is not all.

Elaine watches Michael retch, blows up her cheeks and runs to the bathroom ... projectile vomiting the length of that small dark jazz club.

And that is not all.

After everything is mopped, swabbed, sanitized and we are asked to leave, I realize Jane has disappeared.

I find her in the ladies room, on the toilet, leaning against the stall, spittle running down her chin.

And right, that is not all.

Bunched at her ankles are girdle underpants that even young and thin girls wear to keep things from ... jiggling.

I consider just removing them, but even I know that bringing a girl home without her underpants is a bad idea. So I pull up my semi-comatose girlfriend, drape her arms over my shoulders and inch the girdle up over her calves, her knees, her thighs and up up up over her bottom. Then I kneel, bend her over my shoulder, stand, and wobble nonchalantly through the club, up the steep steps, and over to my father's station wagon on Perry Street.

Of course, that is not all.

With our friends safely back in their suburban homes, Ray and I are parked in front of Jane's house, discussing the best way to return the inebriated girl to her parents. One of us, I don't recall who, suggests we install her between the storm and front doors, ring the bell and run.

We both think that is hysterical, but when some divine sobriety appears, we walk the wobbling girl up the flagstone path, ring the bell, and tell Mom that although we warned Jane about the dangers of drinking too much, she just hadn't listened.

And because every story has another story lurking in the shadows, even that is not all.

The following morning, as I stumble bleary-eyed down the stairs at home, my mother looks up and asks brightly, "You kids have fun?"

This is a month before she will learn I am on academic probation for my 1.7 GPA; two months before my long hair and beard will totally obscure my boyish good looks; three months before I will inform my parents that they and their friends are bourgeois capitalist pigs.

But this is now. So with my best Eddie Haskell smile I say, "Life is a bowl of cherries, Mom!"

And she smiles back, knowing in her heart that her kid really is alright.

KATHERINE MAYER

Katherine Mayer is a potty-mouthed, sometimes cynical storyteller, humorist, and activist sharing life as she lives it in Newtown, Connecticut. She is a recent, reluctant inductee to AARP, the co-creator of two quasi-adults and two wannabees, and an aspiring writer with the rejections to prove it. She is sometimes funny on Instagram and Twitter as @KLMcopy, has invisible friends on Facebook, and writes about teenagers, midlife, social issues, feminism, and gun violence prevention.

CONDOM SENSE

Katherine Mayer

There's a Costco-sized box of condoms in our hall closet, opened, right up front, with a handful removed so nobody's keeping track of how many go missing. Easy access, no questions asked. I want the teenagers in my life to shoplift them all day long. Take one. Take two. Just take.

I'd prefer these horny teenagers save it for someone who matters, someone who will love them inside and out, to their very core and soul, and not just until the parents get home. But such perspective takes time, and trial and error, and while that maturation percolates, I want the teens to have all the facts about STIs, pregnancy, responsibility, compassion, accountability—and free and easy access to condoms. Because the only thing safer than a condom is abstinence and well, that preacher done gone home for the day.

The condom brigade began when my kid's very gorgeous friend had girls drooling over him: smart, ripped, funny, and every parent in town loved him. Us included. Way too short for my daughter (says she, not me), so since kindergarten, they were buds.

Just buds.

Which is how I found out about the Purity Promise Card.

"YOUR WHAT?"

"This," he said proudly, handing the card to me. It was his promise to wait to have sex until marriage. Signed by the priest and himself. Said it right there, I WILL WAIT UNTIL MARRIAGE and signed on the dotted line. It was a flimsy piece of pink paper—why pink?—regular printer paper, not even card stock. Wouldn't hold up, I knew it.

This young, naive boy whom I've known since kindergarten, who still climbed trees and played manhunt in our yard, was quickly becoming a smokin' hot teenager who in ninth grade already had upperclassmen jockeying for prom dibs. And only a cheesy sheath of paper to protect him. His brain hadn't caught up to his brawn—yet—but when it did, that card wasn't gonna help.

"Listen," I said, "I want to give you something. Just in case. I'll be right back." I bounded upstairs without a moment to lose—the weekend was fast approaching!

"Mommmmmm!" It started as a low hum and escalated like a fire alarm. "Mom-mom-mom-mom. MOMMMMMMY! DON'T!" My kid's disgust started as a low warning growl, quickly escalating into an emergency broadcast system alerting the boy to the approaching sex-ed tornado coming in. Fast. Take cover.

Which is exactly what I wanted him to do. TAKE COVER.

"Your promise is perfect," I said as I descended the stairs. "Really, it is. But do me a favor: put this in your wallet, would ya buddy? Because with all due respect, some hot summer night in the back of your parent's minivan, that Promise Card is gonna get you in a whole lotta trouble, and this, this here might just save your night. And your life. Keep it? Please? Just in case, you never know. Maybe you'll never need it, but take it. Promises are good, but condoms are a smart back-up plan just in case your promise card gets dry rot or something."

The story got out around town and it wasn't long before they started stopping by, just to say hi. Or pick up a forgotten book. Or cleats. Teenagers. Team mates. Friends. Not-so-much-friends. Boys. Girls. Slowly but surely, the box began emptying. Not all in one weekend, but over the course of high school, clearly somebody was getting something. Safely, thank you very much.

By senior year, most of my daughter's peers knew where to go when promises made might be broken. "Seriously, Mom," she whined. "Do you have any idea how embarrassing it is that everyone comes to me for condoms, and I'm, I'm, I'm a VIRGIN? Agggghhhh. I'm pathetic. This is so stupid."

"Oh honey," I replied. "Patience. It won't be forever. You're going to college, it'll be worth the wait, I promise."

NATASHA HENRICK

Natasha Henrick, a member of Wallkill Valley Writers, is an adjunct biology professor at SUNY Ulster in Stone Ridge, New York, and works as a consultant for the International Public School Network coaching science teachers. She has recently completed her memoir titled, *The Parts of Him I Kept*, excerpts of which were selected by the New York Writers Institute for a memoir writing seminar taught by James Lasdun of Columbia University.

FAR FROM THE TREE

Natasha Henrick

When my father called I was emptying a closet of crafts and games my children had outgrown.

"Tasha, I've been thinking," he said. "How is Cecily doing?" He paused then.

I moved to the foyer, where the late day sun streamed into the room, picturing my father sitting at his desk, a cigarette burning between his fingers, the thin coating of ash surrounding him. A sign of the ruin his mental illness has wrought.

I braced myself for his next question about my daughter. "Is she still dancing?" he finally asked.

"Yes, she's dancing and painting both," I said, relieved.

He cleared his throat. "So I've decided I should take her to see the film, *Black Swan*."

"*Black Swan* is a horror film about a ballet dancer who loses her mind!" I replied, flashing back to the day he took eight-year-old me to see *The Exorcist* "to instruct me in the ways of the devil, and to protect me."

"I don't want her to see *Black Swan*, Dad. Are you crazy?

"I don't know why you won't let me take her," he shot back. "It's an important film."

"I said no . . . and I'm her mother!"

As if in a battle over her moral instruction, he pressed on to the heart of his mission, to the core of his intended spiritual mentoring.

"You know she's schizophrenic," he said, blindsiding me. His tone, which I long ago learned to interpret, suggested that he hoped for her the same insights he was gifted with, and yet who better than he to know the devastation of the diagnosis he pronounced for her?

The fact that schizophrenia usually lies in wait until young adulthood feels like a weight on my shoulders. When Cecily's older sister, Ella, dressed for Halloween in a white dress, and recited Emily Dickinson's *I'm Nobody! Who Are You?* I worried about how deeply she seemed to feel things. Then as our children reached adolescence and did what teens are renowned for—falling apart at the seams, throwing evidence at me, like dirty laundry, to make a case for the world's conspiracy against them—I worried again.

When I'm at my best, I listen and let their anxieties flow like a wash cycle, rinsing out the stains of the day—what children do when they feel safe. At other times I agonized that their feelings of persecution were early signs of some fault in our genes, waiting to take my oldest daughter's beautiful mind to places I can't reach.

One afternoon while sitting at the kitchen island Ella asked, "Since you don't have schizophrenia does that mean I won't have it either?" After the briefest pause, I told her, "Genetic predispositions can skip a generation, but I am confident that you are fine."

"I read that schizophrenia has been connected with drug use," she continued, "so I decided I'm going to stay away from drugs." I didn't tell her that when I was an adolescent I made different choices, and I wondered then, not for the first time, if I was underqualified to be her mother.

If my father had chosen Ella, I might have been less surprised. But identifying Cecily, our youngest, strong-willed dancer, was so unexpected.

"I don't know that she's schizophrenic, and neither do you," I hissed, but I didn't hang up the phone because I was afraid that if anyone knew madness, it was my father.

"If you ever breathe a word of this to either of our daughters, you will never see us again," I said, shaking with murderous adrenalin. I wanted to beat this threat into him with the handset, but most all—more than anything—I wanted him to be wrong, even delusional.

THE REVEREND CARI PATTISON

The Reverend Cari Pattison serves as Associate Minister at the Reformed Church of Bronxville, New York, and as Acting Head of Staff. In addition to ministry, Cari trained as a Jazzercise, yoga, barre, and Pilates instructor, seeking to inspire people in body and spirit. Originally from Kansas City, Kansas, Cari studied English and art at Kalamazoo College and earned her Masters of Divinity at Princeton Theological Seminary. She previously taught eighth-grade English in Missouri, and served a variety of churches and hospitals in Kansas, Kenya, and New Jersey. Cari has blogged for the *Huffington Post*, illustrated the children's book *ABC: Sing With Me,* and is a 2015 recipient of the Kathryn Gurfein Fellowship at The Writing Institute at Sarah Lawrence College.

MOST WANTED

The Reverend Cari Pattison

"Hello, California Cryobank," a woman answers.

Passing people on the sidewalk, making sure there's no one I know, I lower my voice into the phone. "Hi. I need to order more sperm."

"Donor number?" she asks. "14309," I say, like I'm ordering a J. Crew sweater. I purchase three more vials at nearly a thousand dollars a pop.

"Good luck," she says. "I hope one of these works for you."

It's the summer of 2016. I am forty, single, and want to be a mother. My mom and I spent days poring over donor profiles: medical histories, college grades, and childhood photos. In weekly calls home, my parents chime in on two separate receivers, but whenever Mom and I start talking sperm, Dad signs off.

An anonymous online donor is not how a dad dreams his daughter will conceive. And it still may not work. If not, there will be other options: foster care or adoption, mentoring or volunteering. I'm already a doting aunt to three darling toddlers.

But giving birth to my own child was my first choice, one I'd thought about for a while. Five years earlier and newly divorced, I'd frozen my eggs, eleven of which still rent space at the NYU Fertility Center.

Back then I'd seen a billboard advertising egg-freezing. It showed a young woman holding a baby, with a hand-written letter: "Dear Emma at 30, Thanks for giving me the gift of time. Love, Emma at 40."

I'd frozen my eggs in hopes of later fertilizing them with a man I love. But after dating dozens of men, I'd found plenty of cute cafés and bars, but no partner. I told myself that if I got close to 40 with no man in sight, I could try for motherhood on my own.

But after four basic inseminations, I was closing in on 41. So my doctor switched me to IVF: in-vitro fertilization. When the time came to transfer my first "chromosomally normal" XY embryo, I wondered:

Could I really handle being a single mom? Could I afford it, financially and otherwise? Would I have to give up on finding love? As a minister, would I be accepted by the church? Would God be okay with me giving birth to a baby with no father?

And most importantly—*would the kid be alright?*

The research on single-mothers-by-choice said "yes." Other women who'd done it said "yes." But what about for me?

My sperm donor's kindergarten photo showed a mild-mannered face with brown hair and green eyes. In the section labeled "optional," he'd posted pictures of birds, a music playlist, his favorite books, and his mother's recipe for asparagus soup.

He wrote about hiking with friends in high school: how they went searching for wolves at midnight and found a bear instead. He quoted the Apostle Paul: "I can do all things through Christ who strengthens me."

"What inspires me," he said, "is people who aren't afraid to try things that scare them, to take an opportunity they know will be hard, but they're willing to try."

So he tried. And I tried. And the baby died five weeks into the pregnancy.

Days later at the cemetery, under a lone small tree, my friend and I knelt down in the dirt. As the rain fell, we buried a tiny letter to my boy, who never grew bigger than a sesame seed.

The next day my coworker had to take over my church communion liturgy. There was no part of me that could look out and say, "This is my body, broken for you; my blood, shed for you."

My mom and dad ask when I'll try again. Friends ask me the same.

But my body still holds the hollowness of miscarriage. My heart carries the missed attempts, the staggering cost, the never-ending needles, the lingering side effects. After all that, I have only a badge that says "I tried."

So I can't tell you if and when I'll try again. I can't tell you if more kids will come, or by what means, or what they'll be like. I can only tell you how wanted they will be.

JENNIFER MANOCHERIAN

Jennifer Manocherian has been a theater producer for over twenty-five years with many Broadway and off-Broadway credits, and she moonlights as a writer in various mediums. She wrote the book for the musical *Marry Harry*, which was produced at the New York Musical Festival in 2013 and American Theatre Group in 2014. She has also written several screenplays, one of which she produced as a feature film titled "Hudson River Blues." Previously, she was a family therapist and divorce mediator with several articles published in professional journals. She lives in Scarsdale, New York.

SCARE

Jennifer Manocherian

During a Saturday night sleepover, I was reading and acting out a silly kid's book to my grandson Cole, seven, who was seated on my lap in front of a glass coffee table in the living room. Perhaps I jiggled him or he wriggled, whatever the case, Cole slipped out of my grasp. As he fell over, he whacked his forehead hard against the glass edge. His little body went limp, and scarier still, he didn't cry.

"An ice pack," I screamed to my husband. "Get an ice pack." I scooped Cole up and started shaking him, screaming all the while. When he didn't respond, I screamed to my husband again, "Call 911."

Suddenly Cole jerked out of my arms and bolted away. I ran after him, calling to my husband to cancel the call to 911. Cole dashed up the stairs, then across the hall into our bedroom, through it and into the bathroom, locking the door behind him.

I knocked, frantic to see for myself how he was, anxious just to hold him. "Coley, let me in," I pleaded. "I need to see if you are alright."

"Go away," he yelled. "It was your fault. You pushed me

over." What?? No. He couldn't actually think that. Could he?

"It was an accident. You know I'd never ever push you," I said, close to tears.

My equally frazzled husband joined me and started cajoling Cole to open the door with the same result.

"Did you tell 911 not to come?" I asked.

"Once you make the call, they have to come." By now I could hear sirens fast approaching our house so it was a moot point.

Then it occurred to me that I could be in real trouble if Cole told the EMS people that I had pushed him and that he was hiding behind the locked door to protect himself. What to do? Tell Cole to say that it was not my fault, even if he thought it was? I couldn't ask him to lie. But suppose they believed him?

Before I could come up with a plan, I heard the dogs barking, the doorbell ringing, and loud knocking on the door. I went downstairs to open the door to five uniformed men: three policemen and two EMTs. When I started to say that we didn't need them anymore, one of them interrupted me with, "Where is he?"

"He's fine, he's fine," I said, my voice quivering. "It was a false alarm. He accidentally fell off."

"We need to see him, ma'am," another of the men said, brushing past me.

I led all five of them up the stairs, to the bathroom. At first Cole refused to open the door. "Coley, you need to come out," I told him. "There are a few policemen here who need to see that you are okay."

As we waited, I explained as best I could what had happened. Finally with more coaxing, Cole emerged. He stared at all the men, then said, "It was all Grandma's fault."

"Ma'am, we need to speak to your grandson alone a moment," one of the men told me.

My fate was in the hands of a kid, scared by the fall but even more by my reaction to it.

I backed out of the room, my heart pounding. Who would they believe?

Five long minutes later, the door opened. Cole stood between the two men with a kind of a "cat that swallowed the canary" look on his face. He seemed oblivious to the egg-shaped swelling on his forehead.

"Maybe you'd like to get him an ice pack, ma'am," one of the policeman said.

"Yeah, and an ice cream cone," Cole added, trying hard but not successfully to hide a smile from me. "A double scoop of chocolate chip mint."

DEBORAH BATTERMAN

Deborah Batterman is the author of *Shoes Hair Nails*, a short story collection framed around everyday symbols in our world and their resonance in our lives. A native New Yorker, she has worked over the years as a writer, editor, and teaching artist. She is a Pushcart nominee and took third place in the Women's National Book Association 2012 Short Fiction Contest. Her stories and essays have appeared in anthologies as well as various print and online journals, most recently *Every Mother Has a Story, Vol. 2 (Shebooks/ Good Housekeeping)* and *Open to Interpretation: Fading Light* (Taylor & O'Neill). In 2012 she published a digital chapbook of essays, *Because my name is mother.* Her blog recently took a new turn—a collaboration with her daughter in which a dialogue takes place via alternating posts connected thematically. She can't say she invented the word, but a "diablog" it is.

44

MAKING MY DAUGHTER'S BED

Deborah Batterman

I just finished making my daughter's bed. In the normal course of a day's events, this would not be anything worthy of note, it's something mothers do, a way of tidying up. What makes it something to write about is the mere fact that she was here for a visit, ten days' worth. Now she's gone, back to that place she's lived for several years now, the other coast. Sunny L.A. Even I'm surprised at how it just rolls off my tongue when we drop her at the airport, a hug and a kiss: *Safe trip home.*

This is home, too, always will be in that memory bank of hers, an odd image as I write but one so suitable to what we think of in terms of savoring and squandering. When she first left for college, back when the notion of her coming and going had a predictable rhythm, people would ask: How does it feel to have an empty nest? To which I would quip, "My nest isn't empty, it's just a little quieter." Of course, the dog was very much alive and barking and keeping me busy and entertained in the way dogs do. And the dog's presence — what she added to that place we call home — was something my daughter counted on more that anything else during holiday or summer breaks.

The dog is gone, though not my daughter's relentlessness about my need for a replacement. There is no replacing a dog that lived with you for thirteen years. A dog with her very own personality that any other dog would forever be measured against. There is, though, some sense in some people's minds that home, by definition and/or suggestion, needs a dog.

My home does not need a dog as much as it needs a daughter. Her cosmetics bag and toothbrush on the vanity in the bathroom. Her clothes sprawled on the floor of her bedroom. Her complaints about the thermostat being too low. Her nestling under a fleece blanket on the couch in front of the TV, flanked by that mommy/daddy duo she used to refer to, her own shorthand, as "'rents." Her need for me, not to mention the dog, as she falls asleep when she's not feeling so great.

Her unmade bed.

A writer puts down words, intent on expressing some urgent thought, some deep reflection. A week has passed since my daughter went back to that other home of hers. A week during which I read Joan Didion's exquisitely poignant *Blue Nights*. Why I would even choose to read a book ostensibly about a favorite writer recalling moments surrounding the life of her daughter, now gone, seems perverse. And yet it makes all the sense in the world. *When we talk about mortality, she writes, we are talking about our children.*

I head into my kitchen, daylight nearing its end, the sky a twilight blue artists dream of. The moon, pearly yellow, a lone pendant on a chandelier of tree branches. I stand in front of the window, completely riveted by its commanding presence. It's a mid-winter night sparkling with a landscape of snow laced with moon shadows, and everything about this moon calls to mind a picture book I read to my daughter many times when she was young, *Happy*

Birthday, Moon. There is a bear, in this delightful story by Frank Asch, so entranced by the moon he wants to give it a birthday present. Only problem is that he doesn't know when the moon's birthday is, or what to get him. He climbs a tall tree, to have a chat with the moon. No response.

"Maybe I am too far away, thought Bear, and the moon cannot hear me."

MARY CATHERINE BOLSTER

Mary Catherine Bolster grew up in Iowa but not on a farm. She has been writing in one form or another since her first feature column in the *Compass*, her high school paper. With advanced degrees in nursing and medical ethics, she began her career on the clinical faculty of the University of Iowa and has published articles in *Linacre Quarterly* and other medical and ethical journals. As a freelancer, she wrote consumer-oriented articles for regional magazines and national trade publications, and her position as the national director of marketing and education for a health care organization led her to founding her own company. MCB Communications served health-care and not-for-profit clients, specializing in capital campaigns, consumer and medical writing, and public relations. Bolster currently lives in Manhattan and from time to time still yearns for her beloved prairie.

BY HIS SIDE

Mary Catherine Bolster

The back door opens, then slams shut. "Mom?" I glance at the clock. Ten-thirty.

"Great, Ben," I mutter to myself as I get off the couch. My 17-year-old son doesn't break curfew, but it's the first weekend of summer vacation and he's finally, a senior. It's a possibility.

He slumps against the living room wall, his six-foot frame barely visible in the dim light.

"Got hit," he slurs.

"What?" I say, flipping on the hall light.

"Guy grabbed me."

I gasp. His head lists to one side, both hands cradle his face. A steady stream of blood oozes into a dirty towel.

"Can't close my mouth," he mumbles.

"My boy," I whisper as my finger traces the path of a black bruise running from his ear to mid-chin. I carefully wipe away his tears with my T-shirt, turn to brush away my own, and run for the icepack.

I've spent years teaching nursing in major medical centers. But

I'm useless, numb.

"My braces hurt," he says, eyes filled with tears.

Minutes later the orthodontist returns my call. "Why hit Ben?" he asks. "I'd call the cops." He pauses. "This is assault."

"Yes. I… guess it is," I say, my hands shaking.

It's been ten years or nearly that since he and I left Chicago with his older brother and a beloved Springer Spaniel named Alfie, after what both boys called "that awful divorce." I'd landed a job on the University of Pennsylvania's faculty. And after weeks of weighing the pros and cons of another move on my sons, I accepted, hoping I was doing the right thing.

A sandy-haired policeman pulls up minutes later. He checks out Ben's injuries, asks a few questions, writes in his pocket notebook.

"Ma'am, can I see you outside?" he says, hooking his thumbs into his belt. "I had a guy get sucker-punched like this a while back." He looks down, shifts from one foot to the other. "The kid went to bed and never woke up." He starts down the front steps then turns back. "Too bad your boy didn't duck."

I lean against the porch railing, arms crossed, shivering. Was that a defense I should have taught him?

On the way to the ER, Ben starts moaning, holding the leaking ice bag on his jaw. Blood drips onto the car floor. I step on the gas, keeping up a constant patter, lying to him about how everything's going to be alright. Now I'm in crisis mode. Clinical. In charge. But my patient is my boy. My boy is my patient.

The ER's quiet for Saturday night. In minutes, he's on a gurney, Demerol in his veins, dozing off and on. The young doctor slides the X-rays into the light box. "Jaw's broken in two places." He moves closer to me, hands on hips. "Is he in trouble a lot?" Tears well up in my eyes.

I want to scream: *No. Don't you understand? He's a good boy.*

I've kept him safe. Instead, I recite his resume. Student council. Class president. Editor-in-chief of the school paper. Lead role in *Pippin*. He nods, his gaze softens.

"He's lost a lot of blood. I've got to set his jaw to stop it," he says as he fills another syringe with more Demerol.

"Isn't that too much?" I ask, now a nurse, still a mother.

"He's a big guy, you know."

I nod. *A big guy I couldn't protect.*

The physician thrusts Ben's jaw into alignment. My son stiffens, then screams, a fresh line of tears leaving marks on his pale face. I hold his hand, waiting for the opiates to kick in.

The doctor tells me they'll wire his jaw shut tomorrow, takes off his gloves, and leaves.

Later, I collapse onto a cot in Ben's hospital room. I tell myself he's going to be alright. But in the dark, as I begin my watch, I'm not so sure.

EDWARD McCANN

650 is a writer whose features and essays have been published in national magazines and literary journals *(Better Homes & Gardens, Country Living, Gardener, Good Housekeeping, Ladies' Home Journal, the Sun, and more)*. An award-winning television writer/producer and longtime contributing editor at *Country Living,* Ed is a member of New York City based Artists Without Walls and Irish American Writers & Artists. He's written the text for partner Richard Kollath's design books, and he's recently completed a memoir about the search for his missing nephew. His essay, "Pregnant Again," was selected for the anthology, *Listen To Your Mother,* published by Penguin Books in April, 2015. He lives and writes in New York's Hudson River Valley.

FOUR BLUE EYES

Edward McCann

Four bright blue eyes watch me from the opposite side of the breakfast table. I'm playing peek-a-boo with the twins, my nephews Dublin and Finnegan, who, along with their parents, have moved in with my partner Richard and me, all of us rearranging our lives and priorities to become—at least for a time—a mixed, modern, multi-generational family of six.

The boys stare, then squeal and giggle in all the right places. I hide my face behind a napkin, and then drop it to my lap, making a *Surprise!* face. Next, I whip the napkin aside to reveal an angry face. The boys screech with laughter, waving their arms overhead and kicking their legs out in front of them as I cycle through a street mime's interpretations of grief, boredom, and fear. I'm just a gray-haired, goofball uncle, but these little boys think I'm a rock star. They're my best audience ever, and there's no sound in the world like a baby's belly laugh.

On the other hand, a cranky baby can scream until your nerves are in shreds. And if he's screaming while seated in his high chair beside his twin brother, then his brother may join in. Then you have two screaming, crying, coughing babies who simply cannot be comforted: a pair of shrieking car alarms that won't be silenced. With contorted red faces covered in tears and snot and drool, their limbs are outstretched to full extension, prehensile feet rotating at the ankles, hands opening and closing into balled fists. Studying them, it occurs to me as I reach for my wineglass that they are a pair of tiny, screaming, five-pointed stars, looking something like pocket versions of Leonardo da Vinci's Vetruvian man . . . if Vetruvian man wore a diaper.

Each time I enter either of the boys' line of sight, they smile and babble and crawl or toddle toward me, eager to engage. I might be trying to retrieve mail, or walk the dog, or get to an appointment, but if I try to scoot past Finn with wave and a promise that "I'll be right back," his howls of grief can stop me cold.

As Finn wails and sinks to the floor, I drop my keys, shrug off my jacket, and reach down toward his outstretched arms. Finn quiets as I lift him toward me, clamping his little arms around my neck and resting his head on my shoulder. A flood of new emotion washes over me, and I feel myself flush as I rock the boy and stroke his back, feeling his breath warm against my skin. And then, with the best of intentions, I lie to Finn, whispering a promise that I cannot keep.

"I will never, ever leave you," I say.

After my divorce, I made peace with the assumption that children weren't in the cards for me. But this opportunity is a gift beyond measure, and I'm paying close attention, determined to get the most from this time we share. I will sing silly, made-up songs to Finn; I will retrieve the spoon as many times as Dublin drops it, and I will read *Goodnight, Moon* aloud to them both a hundred times before we start *Harry Potter*. I want to help with their homework; I want to teach them card games and how to tie their shoes and how to ride a bike. And I hope to still be here for questions about birds and bees and broken hearts.

For now, though, the boys have started swim lessons at our local YMCA, and each Thursday morning they splash about wearing swim diapers. When you strip away the particulars, my partner Richard and I are simply helping to shape the lives of these two children whom we love, giving them something invisible that they'll carry forward far into their adult lives.

And that's a special kind of immortality.

ACKNOWLEDGMENTS

In addition to the contributors to this volume, we thank the **New Rochelle Council on the Arts** for its generous support of 650, and for stimulating and encouraging the study and presentation of the performing and fine arts. Throughout the year, NRCA sponsors many exhibitions, theatrical productions, dance recitals, film screenings, lectures, and concert series.
NewRochelleArts.org

We thank the **New Rochelle Public Library** for hosting a 650 live event in its beautiful Ossie Davis Theater. The library offers a comprehensive collection that includes retrospective and current materials, up-to-date technology by which information can be accessed, and a wide range of community services and programs tailored to a diverse audience.
nrpl.org

Nancy Manocherian's the cell has supported 650 from its inception. A twenty-first century salon in the heart of New York City, their mission is to support the arts and to incubate new works, and the cell made its beautiful performance space available to 650 as we were finding our way. The cell: To mine the mind, pierce the heart, and awaken the soul.
TheCellTheatre.org

Artists Without Walls was created to inspire, uplift and unite people and communities of diverse cultures through the pursuit of artistic achievement, and has supported and encouraged 650 from its beginnings. Artists Without Walls: No Limits. No Walls. No Boundaries.
ArtistsWithoutWalls.com

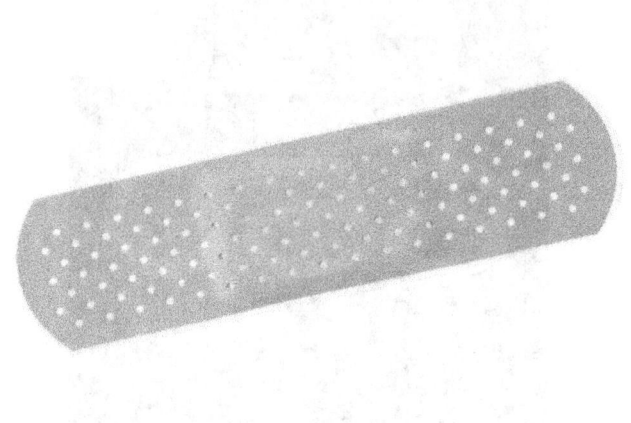